To: Coach Alan Buchanan

From: FEA

11-16-00

TRUTH FOR THE PICKING

HOME·GROWN WISDOM COLLECTION

TRUTH FOR THE PICKING

Original Insights on Life from America's Heartland

PETER REESE

TRUTH FOR THE PICKING

HOME·GROWN WISDOM COLLECTION

The cover features Lucy and Ethel, their work, the author, and his well-traveled laptop.

Photography by Kristen Boom

Copyright © 1997 by Peter Reese

Published by Garborg's Heart 'n Home, Inc.
P.O. Box 20132, Bloomington, MN 55420

All rights reserved. No part of this book may be reproduced in any form without permission in writing from the publisher. Printed in USA.

ISBN 1-881830-50-0

TRUTH FOR THE PICKING

HOME·GROWN WISDOM COLLECTION

The author, a small-scale farmer whose priorities are faith, family, and friends, dedicates this Collection to all readers seeking SIMPLICITY, SIGNIFICANCE, and SECURITY.

The reader is encouraged to laugh, contemplate, and compare experiences—and be ready to offer a differing point of view somewhere along the way.

TRUTH FOR THE PICKING

HOME·GROWN WISDOM COLLECTION

Genius is extraordinary clarity about the ordinary.

TRUTH FOR THE PICKING

HOME·GROWN WISDOM COLLECTION

Simplification is often one of the most complicated tasks.

TRUTH FOR THE PICKING

HOME·GROWN WISDOM COLLECTION

*No destination justifies
a journey without joy.*

TRUTH FOR THE PICKING

HOME·GROWN WISDOM COLLECTION

*Choose your course,
not by signposts but
by destination.*

TRUTH FOR THE PICKING

HOME·GROWN WISDOM COLLECTION

A few good decisions far outweigh dozens of poorly made ones.

TRUTH FOR THE PICKING

HOME·GROWN WISDOM COLLECTION

Living in the fast lane means any flat could be fatal.

TRUTH FOR THE PICKING

HOME·GROWN WISDOM COLLECTION

True power is granted rather than grabbed.

TRUTH FOR THE PICKING

HOME·GROWN WISDOM COLLECTION

*Character not only defines
how we handle a situation but in
which ones we find ourselves.*

TRUTH FOR THE PICKING

HOME·GROWN WISDOM COLLECTION

*Honor.
Given for a lifetime or
lost in a heartbeat.*

TRUTH FOR THE PICKING

HOME·GROWN WISDOM COLLECTION

There is no courage in selfishness, nor bravery in bravado.

TRUTH FOR THE PICKING

HOME·GROWN WISDOM COLLECTION

There is no shame in upholding standards nor prudishness in maintaining principles.

TRUTH FOR THE PICKING

HOME·GROWN WISDOM COLLECTION

Anger is an open flame looking for nearby rubbish to ignite.

TRUTH FOR THE PICKING

HOME·GROWN WISDOM COLLECTION

*Praise those who have many questions.
Pity those who possess only answers.*

TRUTH FOR THE PICKING

HOME·GROWN WISDOM COLLECTION

A legacy is built one choice at a time in the humblest of ways, usually in private.

TRUTH FOR THE PICKING

HOME·GROWN WISDOM COLLECTION

*Simplicity is a decision,
not a result.*

TRUTH FOR THE PICKING

HOME·GROWN WISDOM COLLECTION

To embrace the significant requires us to abandon the empty, spurn the superficial, and flee the frivolous.

TRUTH FOR THE PICKING

HOME·GROWN WISDOM COLLECTION

The fact that lying is so easy is what makes honesty so hard.

TRUTH FOR THE PICKING

HOME·GROWN WISDOM COLLECTION

Caution is mandatory when few boundaries appear to be present.

TRUTH FOR THE PICKING

HOME·GROWN WISDOM COLLECTION

Setting standards requires a desire to say "yes" as well as "no".

TRUTH FOR THE PICKING

HOME·GROWN WISDOM™ COLLECTION

No bottom line justifies crossing the fine lines.

TRUTH FOR THE PICKING

HOME·GROWN WISDOM COLLECTION

*Adventure.
The great, unsteady
leap forward.*

TRUTH FOR THE PICKING

HOME·GROWN WISDOM COLLECTION

Progress.
The small, humble steps
taken consistently.

TRUTH FOR THE PICKING

HOME·GROWN WISDOM COLLECTION

"Why?"
An exceptional question frequently asked before progress is made or innovation exerted.

TRUTH FOR THE PICKING

HOME·GROWN WISDOM COLLECTION

If more words made life better, all the non-stop talkers would be much happier than at present.

TRUTH FOR THE PICKING

HOME·GROWN WISDOM COLLECTION

Money empowers the purposeful, distracts the deceitful, and benefits the benevolent.

TRUTH FOR THE PICKING

HOME·GROWN WISDOM COLLECTION

Without the dreamers, the doers would be lost. Without the doers, the dreamers would lose their role.

TRUTH FOR THE PICKING

HOME·GROWN WISDOM COLLECTION

Honor those who seek none.
Credit those who demand little.
Reward those whose
needs are few.

TRUTH FOR THE PICKING

HOME·GROWN WISDOM COLLECTION

Practice doesn't guarantee perfection, but laziness is a sure ticket to mediocrity.

TRUTH FOR THE PICKING

HOME·GROWN WISDOM COLLECTION

Mastery of the obvious is less elegant, but far more productive, than expertise with the esoteric.

TRUTH FOR THE PICKING

HOME·GROWN WISDOM COLLECTION

A willingness to sacrifice today is what brings fall's harvest and winter's provisions.

TRUTH FOR THE PICKING

HOME·GROWN WISDOM COLLECTION

Some may choose to guess. Others, however, have elected to extrapolate from intuition.

TRUTH FOR THE PICKING

HOME·GROWN WISDOM COLLECTION

Indulgence, when practiced with fervor and frequency, becomes disappointment, despair, and destruction.

TRUTH FOR THE PICKING

HOME·GROWN WISDOM COLLECTION

*Anyone can be busy.
Few are focused enough
to be truly effective.*

TRUTH FOR THE PICKING

HOME·GROWN WISDOM COLLECTION

*Search for your passion
until you discover it.
Once found, hold fast
and don't lose it.*

TRUTH FOR THE PICKING

HOME·GROWN WISDOM COLLECTION

Money is one of the most overvalued commodities on the market.

TRUTH FOR THE PICKING

HOME·GROWN WISDOM COLLECTION

We always have priorities, even when we can't list them.

TRUTH FOR THE PICKING

HOME·GROWN WISDOM COLLECTION

Freedom is a matter of paying a high price for something invaluable.

TRUTH FOR THE PICKING

HOME·GROWN WISDOM COLLECTION

Guessing.
The art of intuitive ignorance.

TRUTH FOR THE PICKING

HOME·GROWN WISDOM COLLECTION

Trust.
Lawyers and judges don't
create it, they merely verify its
existence or absence.

TRUTH FOR THE PICKING

HOME·GROWN WISDOM COLLECTION

Mirrors are about perception.
X-rays represent reality.

TRUTH FOR THE PICKING

HOME·GROWN WISDOM COLLECTION

*Trust.
Hard to find,
easy to lose.*

TRUTH FOR THE PICKING

HOME·GROWN WISDOM COLLECTION

Trouble finds those who aren't vigilant enough to avoid it.

TRUTH FOR THE PICKING

HOME·GROWN WISDOM
COLLECTION

Simplicity.
Setting aside the many
in order to gain any.

TRUTH FOR THE PICKING

HOME·GROWN WISDOM COLLECTION

Pragmatism, carried to its extreme, substitutes results for relationships, effect for affect.

TRUTH FOR THE PICKING

HOME·GROWN WISDOM COLLECTION

*Resolve takes a dream,
turns it into tangible steps,
then takes one without hesitation.*

TRUTH FOR THE PICKING

HOME·GROWN WISDOM COLLECTION

Coincidence happens more often to those who are prepared for it.

TRUTH FOR THE PICKING

HOME·GROWN WISDOM COLLECTION

Time can be given, lost, or misplaced, but never returned.

TRUTH FOR THE PICKING

HOME·GROWN WISDOM COLLECTION

*It is easier to talk than do.
Harder to keep doing than stop.
More difficult still to stop
before going too far.*

TRUTH FOR THE PICKING

HOME·GROWN WISDOM COLLECTION

Confusion is often an overabundance of opinions without any standard for evaluating them.

TRUTH FOR THE PICKING

HOME·GROWN WISDOM COLLECTION

*Concern minimizes problems.
Worry multiplies them.*

TRUTH FOR THE PICKING

HOME·GROWN WISDOM COLLECTION

People of integrity aren't afraid to pick up ringing phones.

TRUTH FOR THE PICKING

HOME·GROWN WISDOM COLLECTION

Political debates turn regular folks into experts and experts into fools.

TRUTH FOR THE PICKING

HOME·GROWN WISDOM COLLECTION

Making a decision takes little courage. Living with the consequences does.

TRUTH FOR THE PICKING

HOME·GROWN WISDOM COLLECTION

The right decisions are often made when no other course of action is possible.

TRUTH FOR THE PICKING

HOME·GROWN WISDOM COLLECTION

No one knows so little as a know-it-all.

TRUTH FOR THE PICKING

HOME·GROWN WISDOM COLLECTION

Anyone can believe in something that costs nothing, offers everything, and asks nothing.

TRUTH FOR THE PICKING

HOME·GROWN WISDOM COLLECTION

*Lighthouses show
how singleness of purpose
prevents multiple disasters.*

TRUTH FOR THE PICKING

HOME·GROWN WISDOM COLLECTION

Adversity.
The best time to dull your pride
and sharpen your skills.

TRUTH FOR THE PICKING

HOME·GROWN WISDOM COLLECTION

Under pressure, some go to pieces. Others find those they've misplaced for years.

TRUTH FOR THE PICKING

HOME·GROWN WISDOM COLLECTION

The greatest obstacles are planned by stubbornness, built from pride, and maintained with anger.

TRUTH FOR THE PICKING

HOME·GROWN WISDOM COLLECTION

*Hard lessons come with high tuition.
Get the most from every course
the first time.*

TRUTH FOR THE PICKING

HOME·GROWN WISDOM COLLECTION

People of integrity aren't afraid to look in the mirror.

TRUTH FOR THE PICKING

HOME·GROWN WISDOM COLLECTION

Flexibility is appreciation for the obvious, preparedness for the overlooked, and anticipation of the impossible.

TRUTH FOR THE PICKING

HOME·GROWN WISDOM COLLECTION

Excuses.
As numerous as grains of sand
on the beach, they are often
laboriously shaped into castles—
and quickly demolished
when the tide rises.

TRUTH FOR THE PICKING

HOME·GROWN WISDOM COLLECTION

*Moments of rest.
Too few in the making,
even rarer in the taking.*

TRUTH FOR THE PICKING

HOME·GROWN WISDOM COLLECTION

We've been warned not to keep the company of fools. Assuming this is true, it's better not to incorporate in the first place.

TRUTH FOR THE PICKING

HOME·GROWN WISDOM COLLECTION

The compass may possess a strong sense of direction, but it is unable to take a single step of the journey alone.

TRUTH FOR THE PICKING

HOME·GROWN WISDOM COLLECTION

*All reputations are earned.
Let yours hold its value over time.*

TRUTH FOR THE PICKING

HOME·GROWN WISDOM COLLECTION

*Ridicule.
A condition which frequently
afflicts true innovators.*

TRUTH FOR THE PICKING

HOME·GROWN WISDOM COLLECTION

Beware of those who claim they are honest, aren't ticklish, or have never been sick a day in their life.

TRUTH FOR THE PICKING

HOME·GROWN WISDOM COLLECTION

Strength is not an absence of weakness but a recognition of its purpose.

TRUTH FOR THE PICKING

HOME·GROWN WISDOM COLLECTION

*Warm kitchens nourish souls
and feed friendships.*

TRUTH FOR THE PICKING

HOME·GROWN WISDOM COLLECTION

The quickest way to find yourself is to locate the nearest mirror.

TRUTH FOR THE PICKING

HOME·GROWN WISDOM COLLECTION

The most direct route is not necessarily the most scenic.

TRUTH FOR THE PICKING

HOME·GROWN WISDOM COLLECTION

The cost of peace is the surrender of pride.

TRUTH FOR THE PICKING

HOME·GROWN WISDOM COLLECTION

*Humor may not save a life
but it can preserve one's sanity
in times of turmoil.*

TRUTH FOR THE PICKING

HOME·GROWN WISDOM COLLECTION

Resist the temptation to serve as the devil's advocate: He's already got enough help, thank you.

TRUTH FOR THE PICKING

HOME·GROWN WISDOM COLLECTION

Choose a path, not because it's well worn, but because its destination is your own.

TRUTH FOR THE PICKING